The Millionaire's Handbook

Peter Eldin

The Millionaire's Handbook

with drawings by Roger Smith

An Armada Original

The Millionaire's Handbook was first published in
Armada in 1982 by Fontana Paperbacks,
14 St. James's Place, London SW1A 1PS

© Eldin Editorial Services 1982

Printed in Great Britain by Love & Malcomson Ltd.,
Redhill Road, Redhill, Surrey.

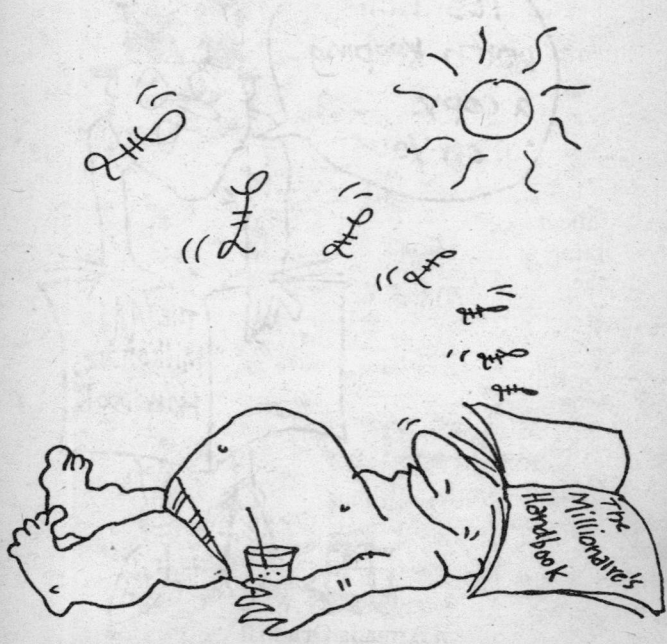

Contents

Introduction

Have you noticed that no matter how much pocket money you get it never seems to go very far? They say that money talks but all it ever seems to say is "good-bye". No doubt you have often wished that your mum and dad could give you more. But not many mums and dads are millionaires so the amount they can afford to give you is usually limited. Instead of always relying on them, why don't you do something about it yourself?

You could, for example, look in your local newspaper for a part-time job. Or when you see a poster outside a police station saying "Murderer wanted" you could perhaps apply for the post!

Another possibility is to move to Jeopardy. I do not know where it is but there must be plenty of work there, for union leaders are always saying there are hundreds of jobs in jeopardy.

If these approaches fail then take a look in this book. It will provide you with lots of ideas on how to make money and thus to taking your first step to becoming a millionaire. In a book of this size it is not possible to give details of *every* way to make some extra money. To do that would require a set of encyclopedias. But I hope that this selection will give you some indication of the hundreds of things you can do to make yourself richer.

If, as a result of trying any of the ideas, you do become a millionaire and you chance to see a poor dishevelled figure selling matches on a street corner, take pity and give him a few pounds. It is probably me.

Peter Eldin

Cash From Household Chores

Here is a good way to make a lot of money from doing a few household chores—if you can get your mother to fall for it. Offer to do thirty jobs around the house. When your mother has recovered from the shock you tell her that you expect to be paid.

She will naturally ask how much you want and you say that for the first job you will charge only ½p. This will give her another shock! She will be even more surprised when you say that for the second job you will charge only 1p, for the third 2p, and for the fourth 4p. You further explain that for each subsequent job you will continue to charge only twice the price of the previous job.

To your mother it may sound like a bargain of a lifetime. But just hope that she does not bother to work it out for it is amazing how quickly the price mounts up using this system. By the time you reach the thirtieth job she will be rather broke for it will be worth £2,684,354.56!

The total you will receive for all the jobs (if you are lucky!) will be a staggering £5,368,709.11½! Just think how long it would take you to count that lot!

Mum's out for the count!

£5,368,709.11½
Soon as poss.

Double Your Money

Seven ways you could double your pocket money:

1. Buy a packet of seeds, plant them, and sell the produce.

2. Fold a £1 in half. It is now doubled.

3. Buy some shampoo, polish, and dusters. Use them to clean a neighbour's car (see page 84).

4. Buy an orange, some cloves, and a ribbon. Push the cloves into the orange until it is completely covered. Leave on a windowsill to dry out. Now tie a ribbon around the orange and sell it as a sweet-smelling pomander.

5. Buy some butter, caster sugar, eggs and self-raising flour. Make a tray of small cakes and sell them to friends.

6. Put some paper money in your pocket. Leave it there for a while. When you take it out you will find it in creases.

7. Buy some flour and yeast. Mix them with water. You now have plenty of dough!

Money of the Mind

This is a good trick with money that will convince your friends you can read minds. While you are out of the room someone places any English coin on the table and covers it with an ordinary tea cup. You then come back into the room and tell everyone the value of the coin hidden underneath the cup and whether it is heads or tails uppermost!

To do this amazing trick you need a friend who knows how the trick is done. It is he or she who places the cup over the coin. This looks natural but it is done in a special way. Before your show you both learn the code shown in the illustration. The way the cup handle points tells you the value of the coin.

If you imagine the handle of the cup to be like the hand of a clock and it is pointing to twelve o'clock you know the coin is a 50p. For a 5p coin your accomplice will place the handle so it points to eight o'clock and so on. The front edge of the table

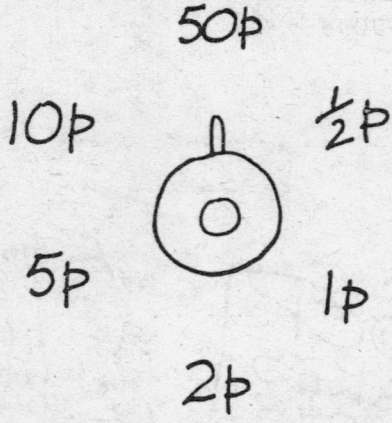

is the top of your imaginary clock face. (If you are performing this trick with coins of a different currency, it will not prove too difficult to devise an appropriate code.)

When someone puts a coin on the table your secret assistant pops the cup over it so the handle is in the correct position. When you come into the room you glance at the cup and you know immediately what value the coin underneath is.

And how do you know if the coin is heads or tails uppermost? Just take a quick look at your friend as you enter the room. If he has one hand in his pocket the answer is "tails". If he has both hands in his pockets then the coin has the head side uppermost.

I know how to handle this problem...

When You Are Left Holding The Baby

A useful way of earning extra cash is to go out babysitting. (This does not mean that you sit on a baby.) In many cases there will be more than one baby to look after and very often you will find that the baby is not a baby at all but a child of anything up to a few years younger than yourself.

One advantage of babysitting as a job is that you can usually do something else at the same time (provided that the baby will let you). While babysitting you could be making dolls for sale, writing articles for magazines, or doing your homework. Whatever second job you choose to do, make sure it is clean. You will not be asked to babysit again if you spend your time repairing a dirty, greasy bicycle in the living room!

If you like children and responsibility, babysitting can be quite enjoyable—until the kids start bawling their heads off, the water pipes burst, and the television explodes!

Here are a few tips for trouble-free (well almost!) babysitting:

1. Before taking on a new babysitting job ask the parents if you can meet the children. This will help them get to know you so you will not be a complete stranger when their parents go out to play bingo.

2. Always turn up on time. The parents are going out for a reason and they may have to be somewhere at a particular time. Make sure you are prompt and you will not make them late.

3. If for any reason you are unable to babysit (mumps, World War Three, cowardice, . . .) let the parents know as soon as possible. If you can, suggest the name of a friend who will take over from you.

4. Before the parents go out, ask for a telephone number where they can be contacted in an emergency.

5. Find out as much as possible about the children's routine. This will not only make your job a lot easier but it will also impress the parents with your sincerity and professional approach. If you are babysitting in the evening, ask what time the children go to bed, whether they like to take any cuddly toys (such as hand grenades) with them, if they have a drink before bed, a light left on, and so on.

6. Respect other people's privacy and property. Many parents will allow you the freedom of the house and the equipment in it. This is all very nice provided that you do not abuse their hospitality by telephoning your cousin in Peru, have the television blaring, and raid the fridge for a six-course banquet.

Ask the parents if you can meet the children.

7. Be prepared to play with the baby or to tell older children stories. Do not forget you are babysitting for the benefit of the parents and their children, and not just for yourself. Their needs and interests must always come first.

8. Keep an eye on the children. Too many babysitters think that all the job entails is watching television. Even if the kids are asleep check them from time to time to make sure all is well.

Keep an eye on the children.

9. Although they may not have horns, children, both young and old, can be little devils. But you must never lose your patience. They are in your care. Try to be patient, friendly, but firm in your dealings with them and they will come to respect you and do exactly as they are told (you hope!).

It's a Fact!

The term "Piggy bank" has got nothing whatsoever to do with pigs. It comes from the name of a ceramic material called "pygg" which was used to make souvenirs and other cheap objects. Because of the name it was only natural that it would eventually be used to make little pigs.

At one time the ancient Greeks used oxen for money. Smaller units of money were represented by calves, sheep, and heifers. Cattle was used as a currency in many other parts of the world and it is from this use that we get our terms "heads" and "tails" for coins. The use of cattle as money has also given rise to the modern word "fee" which comes from "fe", the old Norse word for "cattle".

The film actor W. C. Fields was so afraid of losing his money that he opened a bank account whenever he had loose change in his pocket. He opened hundreds of accounts all over America. Because he used false names and never kept a record of them, many of the accounts remain open to this day, even though Fields died in 1946.

British coins carry the letters D. G. REG. F. D. alongside the Queen's portrait but very few British people notice them. Even fewer know they stand for the Latin words "Dei Gratia, Regina, Fidei Defensor" which means "By the Grace of God, Queen, Defender of the Faith".

Ghost Coin

One thing most people find true about money is that it disappears very quickly. This ghost coin vanishes even faster.

Just hold two coins between the tips of your forefingers. Now rub the coins up and down very briskly against each other.

If you watch very closely you will see a third coin appear between the two coins.

It really does look as if you have three coins but as soon as you stop rubbing, the ghost coin disappears—just like your pocket money!

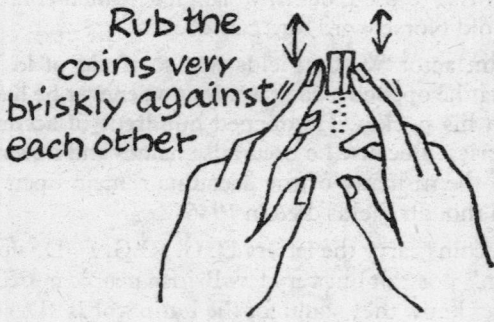

Rub the coins very briskly against each other

It's a Snappy Business

Photography is a great hobby—it can also be a very good way of earning extra money. If you are a good photographer you can offer your services for birthday parties, outings, weddings, and many other occasions. You may also be able to sell your pictures to newspapers and magazines.

Photographs can also be used to make Christmas cards, calendars, place mats, and a wide range of other useful gifts.

One snag with setting yourself up as a photographer is the high cost of equipment. It is, however, possible to start with simpler, less expensive equipment and to gradually improve it as your skills and your sales increase.

Make sure your name and address is on the back of every photograph. It could help you to get more jobs. Don't use a ball point pen for this as it causes indentations and the print will no longer be usable. The best method is to have a rubber stamp made at a stationer's shop. It should cost less than £4 (the stamp not the shop).

In addition to taking photographs for other people and selling photographs, you may also be able to add to your income by entering photographic competitions—provided, of course, that you win.

19

Getting Crafty

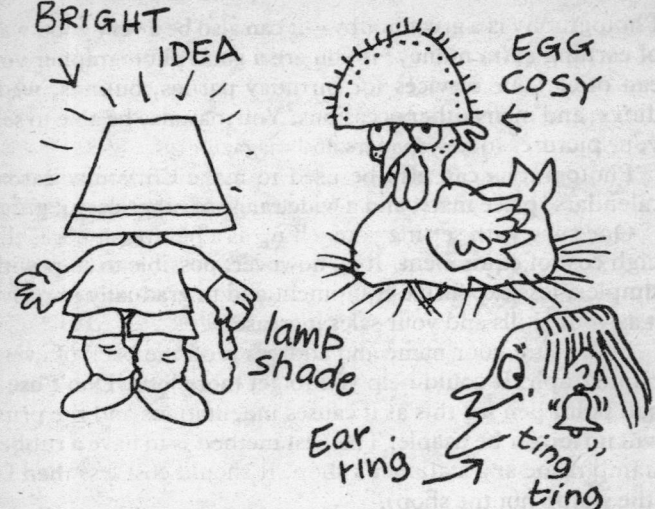

If you are any good at making things, you have a good chance of finding a profitable market for your product. If you make attractive dollies, wooden toys, egg cosies, doll's clothes, or whatever, there may well be a craft shop or market stall in your area that will be only too pleased to buy them from you.

With craft work, as with all businesses, it is important that you make sure there is a market for your work before you start investing time and money in making things. If your hobby is making trunk muffs for elephants, all well and good. But do not make a hundred and hope to sell them. Make just one or two and take them along to your craft shop or sell them to friends. If there is a demand you will be asked to make some more and you may then have the startings of what could develop into a successful business.

There are many crafts that can be made into profitable businesses and it would be impossible to mention them all. Some ideas, such as making candles, jewellery, lampshades, and so on are mentioned in this book but there are hundreds of other crafts you could try.

Let There Be Light

There is a constant demand on anyone who can make decorative candles cheaply and effectively. That someone could be you, for you do not have to be either a bright spark or a flaming idiot to make candles that sell.

It is possible to buy candle-making kits, but it is fairly easy to make your own candles without a kit. First you will need some special moulds—or you can use plastic bottles or cartons instead.

Gently melt some paraffin wax (obtainable from a craft shop) in an old pan. Great care must be taken at this point for the wax can burst into flame very easily. It is as well to have a member of the local fire brigade standing by just in case. Part of a colouring disc (from the same shop) is then melted into the wax.

Allow the wax to cool.

As it cools, a crust will form on its surface. Break this up with a wooden spoon. Leave the wax for a little longer and then again break up the crust. Continue this process until the wax attains the consistency of thick porridge (but do not try eating it for breakfast!).

Wipe the inside of your mould with a solution made from equal parts of glycerine and washing-up liquid. This will prevent the wax from sticking. A special mould-release spray can be bought for this job if you wish.

Push a length of wick through a small hole in the base of the mould and tie a knot on the outside. Drape the other end of the wick over the top edge of the mould and then pour in the wax. Pull the wick to the centre of the wax when the mould is full and it should remain in position.

Allow the wax to set.

When the wax has set, cut the knot from the end of the wick and tip the candle from the mould. If it does not come out easily put it in a refrigerator for half an hour and then try again.

To give your candle a smooth, professional finish, dunk it in boiling water for an instant—but mind your fingers. Trim each end of the wick and your candle is ready for sale.

With practice you will be able to make multi-coloured candles, perfumed candles, and hand-moulded candles. You could also make original candles for special occasions—decorated with nursery rhyme characters for children's parties, with horseshoes and silver decorations for weddings, and with holly for Christmas, all of which will make useful and profitable additions to the range of candles you sell.

Wedding
Cake
decorations

(Watch them
melt into
each
other's
arms)

Two things to remember:

1. If you make candles never upset your customers. You may get on their wick.

2. Do not make a mess with the wax in your mother's kitchen or she may give you some whacks!

How To Run a Successful Business

To start your own business requires hard work, determination, and a certain amount of luck if it is to be successful. You will, however, find it a little easier if you take note of the following points.

1. Satisfy a need. Look around in your area and try to establish what product or service is likely to be needed by a large number of people who live there. If you can satisfy that need with your business you will be giving yourself a good chance of success.

2. In deciding what your business is to be, try to make full use of any talents, interests, or hobbies you may have. It is much easier to run a business if you know something about it to start with and if you enjoy what you are doing.

It is much easier to run a business if you enjoy what you are doing . . .

3. Advertise. The best form of advertising is word of mouth. If you are good at your job and courteous to your

I'M THE GREATEST

The greatest what?

The best form of advertising is word of mouth

customers the word will soon spread around your neighbourhood (and perhaps even further afield) and you will begin to receive requests for your services. Initially, however, it may be necessary to advertise your business in the local newspapers or by means of a card in a shop window.

4. Be prepared to work hard.

5. Learn as much as you can about your business so you can advise your customers and thus give them a better service.

6. Keep records. You should keep a record of all the work you do so you can refer to it if need be. It is also worthwhile keeping a record of all your customers. This can easily be done in a small card index, with a card for each customer on which you record his or her name and address, personal details that may be relevant to your business, and any particular likes or dislikes.

Mighty Oaks From Little Acorns

Do not be downcast at the thought of starting your business in a small way. Many of today's most successful companies started right at the bottom. And, after all, everybody has to start somewhere.

FLEAS FOR SALE

Catch 'em yourself.

The fortune of shipping magnate Daniel K. Ludwig was once estimated to be in excess of three billion dollars. His business career started when he bought a wrecked boat that everyone said could not be saved. He had the boat raised, fixed it himself, and then chartered it out. He made a one hundred per cent profit within one year. He was nine years old at the time.

BOAT FOR HIRE

The world-wide travel service offered by Thomas Cook's was started in 1841 when Thomas Cook, secretary of the Leicester Temperence Movement, chartered a train to take a party from Leicester to Loughborough, a mere ten miles (16km).

When Billy Butlin arrived in England for the first time he had only a few pounds in his pocket. He set up a small hoop-la stall and from that small beginning the famous Butlin's Holiday Camp empire was born.

Aristotle Onassis, the Greek shipping millionaire, who, in addition to a fleet of tankers, owned hotels, land, banks, and the Greek national airline was, in 1922, employed by the telephone company in Buenos Aires, Argentine for 25 cents per hour. Eight years later he was a millionaire importing tobacco.

Michael Marks, a young Polish emigree, sold goods from door to door when he first arrived in England. After a while he had progressed to owning a small market stall in Leeds. Before long he had several such stalls in surrounding districts. The price of everything offered on his stalls was just one penny (½p) and this went down well with his customers who were even poorer than he was. In 1890, six years after starting his first market stall, he had five of his Penny Bazaars operating. At this point he wished to expand further but he did not have the money to do so. He was introduced to a young cashier, Samuel Spencer, and six days later on 22nd September, 1894, the now famous firm of Marks and Spencer was founded.

Henry Ford, who created the now famous Ford Motor Corporation, began his career making motor cars in his garden shed.

When he died in 1877, Cornelius Vanderbilt was reckoned to be the richest man in America. He had amassed a fortune in the region of $100 million which, even by today's standards, is a great deal of money. His business empire began at the age of sixteen when he bought a small boat with money borrowed from his parents and began ferrying people between Staten Island and New York City.

Foyles, now the largest bookshop in the world, started when two brokers began selling the books they had used as students.

The famous stamp firm of Stanley Gibbons began with Edward Stanley Gibbons' fascination with stamps as a schoolboy.

E. STANLEY GIBBONS →

(When he gets angry he still stamps his feet.)

Just think—start your business in a small way today, offer something the public wants, be prepared to work hard, and perhaps one day you too will be a millionaire!

Spot The Forgery

These notes all look the same but one of them is a forgery. Take a good look and see if you can discover which one is different to all the others.

Answer on page 127.

Recycling Cycles

It is amazing how many people have a bicycle and yet have no idea how to look after it or to repair it. Because of this you can establish quite a prosperous business repairing, maintaining, and renovating bikes if you have any mechanical aptitude.

You only need some basic tools—spanners, a screwdriver, tyre levers, and perhaps a hammer. And with a puncture repair outfit, some rags and some paraffin for cleaning you are in business.

For the general routine work you will need to know how to mend a puncture, check the brakes, clean and tighten a chain, how the lights work, how the gears work, and how to lubricate a bike. You will also need to get to know other aspects of bicycle maintenance and if you do not know these things to start with you will find there are several good books available that will tell you what to do.

If you are good at your job you will find that another profitable sideline is obtaining old bikes, often for next to nothing, and renovating them for resale.

you only need some basic tools

Fit Them In

The words listed below are all connected with money or wealth. See if you can fit them all into the grid shown on the opposite page.

4 letters
BANK
CASH
COIN
MINT
RICH

5 letters
MONEY
PURSE

6 letters
CHANGE
CHEQUE

7 letters
BULLION
PREMIUM

8 letters
CURRENCY
TREASURE

11 letters
HIGH FINANCE

Answers on page 127.

Buying and Selling Things

To be a successful buyer and seller you will have to build up a list of contacts, people who are prepared to buy things that you have for sale. Get to know people who collect china, cigarette cards, coins, and so on. Now go along to local jumble sales and look for those items for which you have a possible buyer. You might pick up a packet of old cigarette cards for about 10p and sell them to your collector friend for 75p. It may not sound much but if you have enough people who are prepared to buy such things it is amazing how much you can make.

It will take a while to build up the knowledge you'll need and just as long to achieve a reputation for spotting a bargain. After a while you will get to know about specific items that someone wants and you can then keep a look out for them. It will pay you to specialise so that you gain a knowledge of your subjects. Only in this way will you be able to judge whether or not something is worth what you are asked to pay. The whole success of this type of venture depends upon how much you are prepared to work at finding out what has a potential value and what has not. It must be admitted that this is a very difficult way to make money at first but it is also a most interesting job.

Get to know people who collect things...

Be a Comic Seller

The term "comic seller" does not mean that you have to dress up as a clown and go from door to door selling jokes. It means selling second-hand comics and magazines—something that can develop into quite a lucrative business.

Offer your friends 1p for each of their comics in good condition. You then sell the very same comics to other people for 2p (more if you think you can get it).

You could also offer to pay ½p for the return of each comic you have sold which you will then resell for 2p once again. To identify the comics with which you have dealt, mark them with a rubber stamp or put your signature on the front page.

Only deal in comics and magazines that are in good condition. Always check them for tears or missing pages before buying them in the first place.

Some very old comics and magazines have become collectors' items so it is worth while finding out which ones are valuable and keeping a look out for them. It is very satisfying to buy a comic for 1p and then sell it to a collector for £5!

Check the Rules

There are several rules and regulations governing young people at work. These rules may prove to be annoying at times but they were designed to protect you. No longer can children be sent up chimneys, down mines, or employed for excessive hours on dangerous jobs as was the practice in the past.

No longer can children be sent on dangerous jobs

Unfortunately, the laws governing young people at work are complicated by the fact that there are also local bye-laws covering the same subject. To find out what the law is in your part of the world ask your local youth employment officer, citizen's advice, or library. They should be able to help.

As a general rule it should be remembered that most local authorities will only permit 13 and 14 year-olds to work a total of 25 hours a week. When you are 15 or 16 these hours are increased to 35. During school holidays you will not be allowed to work for more than five hours each day. And while you are at school the limit is one hour before school (but not before 6am and not after 8am) or two hours after school. If you are under 13 it is against the law for someone to employ you except in some light agricultural work and some aspects of stage work. There is, however, nothing to stop you from starting your own business venture.

In addition to checking with the authorities you should also let your parents know what you intend to do. It is possible that they may not like the idea so you will not be able to do it (for you always do what your parents say, don't you?). Even if your parents do not mind they have the right to know what you are up to. And there is always the possibility that you will earn too much and adversely affect the amount of income tax that your parents have to pay (the amount you can earn without affecting your parents' income tax position is announced in the budget statement each year. In the 1982 budget this was fixed at £1,565 per year (£30.00 a week) but is likely to change in subsequent budgets).

Your teachers should also know of your plans. If the school thinks that your work will interfere with your education they may ask you not to do it.

Rules of Selling

Whilst there is nothing to stop you selling things privately from your own garden (apart from your parents) there are all manner of restrictions that will hamper, or even prevent, you once you go outside the garden gate and on to the public highway. You could be prosecuted for selling without a licence, causing an obstruction, or even for vagrancy. If you are selling garden produce or other foods you become involved in health rules and regulations that are extremely complicated. If your business is conducted on a small scale then the extra frustration of "going official" is generally more trouble than it's worth. If, however, you do expand your business to the stage where you have to move off private property then you must contact your local council and your local health inspector first.

Funny Money

Why does a lifeguard have a lot of money?
Because he is always saving.

What is a millionaire's favourite soup?
Moneystrone.

What is a billionaire's favourite meal?
Sausages and cash.

What do you call someone with a pound note in his ear?
A cashier.

What did Hamlet say when he saw a coin on the ground?
2p or not 2p that is the question.

How do millionaires end a friendly game of chess?
With the words "cheque mate".

What sort of money is found in the ocean?
Curren-sea.

What sort of holiday do rich people have when they get married?
A moneymoon.

Why are millionaires musical?
Because they always have plenty of notes.

Why are millionaires good bakers?
Because they've always got plenty of dough.

Carrying the Bag

Shopping for other people may not sound very interesting but it can prove a valuable service for the housebound, the elderly, and the busy housewife.

Always get a written list of the things wanted. As you buy each item, tick it off the list and write the price alongside. (In addition to listing the prices, keep all the till receipts from each shop you visit so everything can be checked.)

Put solid items in the bottom of the shopping bag and squashy items on top. It is no good buying strawberries only to have them squashed to a pulp in the bottom of the bag.

Keep soap powders and the like away from food items wherever possible.

When you return to the house give your customer the original list and the receipts, together with the correct change.

Count out the change and make sure the person watches you do it (see page 53). Some people will say there is no need to do this as they trust you. But whether they trust you or not, still make a point of doing it. It may save arguments later. Incidentally, you should also ask your customer to write down how much they are giving you before you go out so no mistakes are made.

Count the change and make
sure the person watches you

If the bulk of your shopping is to be done in one area, get to know the prices each shop charges. Most customers will be very pleased when you point out that you bought the sugar in a particular shop because it was two pence cheaper than the other shops. You will find that if you make several purchases at the cheapest price possible you can save your customer quite a bit of money.

If you use a string or wicker bag and the shopping is heavy, tie a roller skate to the bottom. You can then wheel the shopping along instead of carrying it. It can be a bit awkward going up and down steps but it is better than having your arms stretched by heavy bags.

For small amounts of shopping, charge a small set fee of about 30p. If there is to be a lot of shopping then you could suggest a fee of ten per cent of the shopping bill. So, if the shopping amounts to £5 you can charge 50p. For heavy shopping you could perhaps charge a little more. If your customers are old or not very well off then perhaps you should charge a little less. But whatever you charge, make sure you agree the price with your customer before you actually do any shopping.

Going Crackers

Making Christmas crackers is not so crackers as it may sound. It can be a profitable business especially as shop-bought crackers are often expensive.

Tools required:
Scissors, two paper tubes (from inside kitchen rolls).

Materials required:
Coloured crepe paper, tissue paper, thin card, cotton, glue, jokes, small gifts, snaps (or bangs), motifs (shapes of animals and so on cut from old birthday and Christmas cards and gummed paper shapes).

Jokes
Type some jokes on small slips of paper. Hundreds of suitable jokes can be found in Armada joke books.

Gifts
These can be bought from toyshops or newsagents. If you plan to make a lot of crackers it is cheaper to buy your gifts in quantity at wholesale prices. Firms that sell small gifts regularly advertise in magazines such as *The World's Fair* and *Exchange & Mart*. L. Davenport & Co., of 51 Great Russell Street, London W.C.1 can also supply a wide range of novelties.

Snaps
Snaps are available from L. Davenport & Co. (address above), Reliance Snap Co. Ltd., Twyford Road, Bishops Stortford, Herts. or from Stoneleigh Mail Order Co., 19 Prince Avenue, Southend on Sea. SS2 6RC.

To make a cracker
  1. Place a piece of crepe paper measuring about 25 cms x 18 cms flat on your table.

2. Put a sheet of tissue paper measuring slightly less than the crepe paper on top.

3. Lay down the snap, place a joke near to the centre of the snap, and put a piece of thin card about 2 inches (5 cms) long in the centre.

4. Place the two cardboard tubes, end to end, on top of the papers. Roll the paper layers up around the tubes (which act as formers) and glue them into position.

5. Pull the right tube out of the cracker about 5 cms to the right. Tie a length of cotton around the cracker at the gap formed between the two tubes and pull it tight.

6. Remove the right hand tube.

7. Drop the gift into the end of the second tube and then pull this out a short way. Tie another piece of cotton around the cracker at the same distance from the end as the first length of cotton.

8. Remove the left hand tube.

Your cracker is now complete apart from any decorative motif you may decide to glue to the outside to make it look more attractive. Special motifs can be put on crackers for birthday parties, weddings, and other celebrations — for crackers do not have to be restricted only to Christmas.

And with your crackers any party is bound to go off with a bang.

Be a Collector

Collecting things is sometimes a good way of making money. Unfortunately you usually have to wait a long time for the thing you have collected to increase in value, and there is never any guarantee that this will actually happen. The big problem is knowing in advance what items that are perhaps commonplace today are going to be the sought-after items of tomorrow. In most instances, therefore, you should look upon collecting as a hobby rather than your opportunity to become a millionaire, and only collect things in which you have an interest. If you're lucky, the beer mats, newspapers, or pickle jars of today may well be collectors' items in the future. The same is true of coins, stamps, gramophone records, or your granny's corsets. Other collecting hobbies that can be turned into profitable businesses include matchboxes, cigarette cards, autographs, cheese labels, and almost anything else you can think of.

When barbed wire was introduced into America it was regarded by many as a nuisance. Nowadays small pieces of old barbed wire have become highly prized collector's items! Which means that virtually anything you collect today could have a value in the future!

Small pieces of old barbed wire have become highly prized collector's items!

The Stamp of Success

If your hobby is stamp collecting then the job of stamp dealer could be the natural thing for you to try.

You can buy or swap stamps from your friends and then sell them to other people. It is a particularly good job if you can discover a source of free stamps (such as your father's office or a foreign pen-pal) as anything you then make from your dealings is pure profit.

Stamps can also be obtained from dealers who specialise in selling stamps in bulk to other dealers. They advertise in most stamp magazines. Some dealers sell kiloware. These are stamps still on paper so you will have to remove them by soaking before you can sell them.

Display the stamps you have for sale in approval books. These hold the stamps in transparent pockets. You could make your own approval books but they can be bought from stamp dealers fairly cheaply and then used over and over again.

The condition of the stamps you sell is most important. Usually, the better the condition the higher the price you can charge. Rarity is another important factor. Many people believe that the 1840 Penny Black of Great Britain, the first stamp to be issued, is the rarest stamp, but this is not the case. The rarest stamp in the world is the one cent magenta issued in British Guiana and post marked "Ap. 4 1856". This stamp was once sold by a schoolboy for just six shillings (30p) because he did not like the look of it. In 1980 that very same stamp changed hands for an incredible £425,000!

It is obviously well worthwhile gaining some knowledge of the stamps you are buying and selling. To help you do this, consult the catalogues which are available from book shops and stamp dealers and can also be seen in your local library.

Like most business, it is your determination that will make this one succeed. Never take any notice of the wit who will tell you that "philately will get you nowhere."

Pence Sense

When you receive payment for your first job, do not immediately rush out and spend it all at once. Just think for a few minutes of what you want to achieve with it, and with all the other money you will soon be earning for other jobs. It will be well worth your while to draw up a budget to give you some idea of what you hope to receive and how you are going to make full use of any money you earn.

The first step in drawing up any budget plan is to find out how you spend your money to start with. To do this, start a budget diary in which you record how much you spend each day and what you spend it on. Keep the diary going for a month or more and then total up everything. You may get quite a surprise when you discover that a great deal of your hard-earned cash is being spent on things you do not really need, such as sweets, chips, hamburgers, and shark's fin-flavoured lollipops.

EXPECTATIONS

8p
Returnable
bottles

Being helpful
(like keeping 50p
out of the way)

OUTGOINGS

2 tickets Wembley
£15.00
cakes 72p
Broken window
I.O.Us £1.33 50p

Using the analysis you have just made, you can plan ahead with your spending. Estimate how much you expect to receive in the coming weeks and list all the necessary expenditure. It is a good idea to over-estimate what you intend to spend and to under-estimate what you expect to receive.

Your forward plan will enable you to see just how much you will have to earn from your business to cover all your expenses. If the planned income is less than your planned expenditure then you must either find some way of increasing your income or reducing your expenditure. One successful way of cutting out all unnecessary spending is to nail all your money to a thick plank of wood. That way you will not be able to spend anything because you cannot budge it.

It is as well to update your budget every six months so you know exactly where you are at all times. It is not a bad idea to keep your budget diary going continuously as you will then have a complete record of what you have received and spent.

When planning ahead with your spending, make sure you put a regular amount away for saving. A little less spent on unnecessary items will result in quite a reasonable nest-egg of money over a period of time. You can never start saving too soon. For, as the monk said as he rushed to get dressed when the monastery fire bell rang, "The quicker you get into the habit, the better."

Quite a reasonable nest-egg

Currency Search

All the different types of money listed below are hidden in the grid on the opposite page. They may be written vertically, horizontally, or diagonally and either backwards or forwards. One has been marked to give you a start. Now see how many of the others you can find.

BAHT
BOLIVAR
CEDI
CORDOBA
CRUZEIRO
DINAR
DOLLAR
DRACHMA
ESCUDO
FORINT
FRANC
GOURDE
GUILDER
KIP
KORUNA
KRONE
KYAT
LEI
LEK
LEMPIRA
LFV

MARK
PESETA
PESO
PIASTRE
POUND
QUETZAL
RAND
RIAL
ROUBLE
RUPEE
RUPIAH
SCHILLING
SOLE
SUCRE
TUGRIK
WON
YEN
YUAN

Currency
search

```
L E K R T O B O L I V A R
O D R A C H M A Y P G T O
D G O R E T A T E S E P U
S U N D D R A B N O D I B
C I E L I S K O R U N A L
H L L P E S O I U H A S E
I D M S O L E E P U R T I
L E V S T Z M N I O O R T
L R U Q U E T Z A L U E B
I G R R G W D G H E R N E
N E C O R D O B A S R D D
G E N R I A L N E C R I R
E N A R K E L C Y U A N U
F O R I N T A Y K D R A O
D E F S U C R E R O E R G
```

Answers on page 127.

Making Money by Magic

With this magic purse you can make money by magic—or at least you can appear to do so.

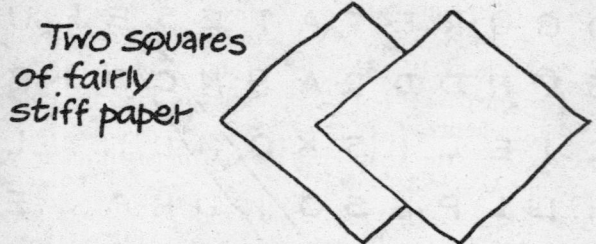

Two squares of fairly stiff paper

All you need is two squares of fairly stiff paper. Fold each piece of paper into three in each direction so that when you open it up the creases form the outline of nine squares as shown in the second illustration.

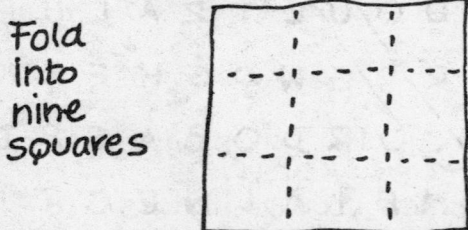

Fold into nine squares

Now fold each piece of paper up as follows. Fold the left edge in and then fold the right side in over the top of it. Next fold the top edge in to the centre and then fold the bottom edge up over it. You should now have two packets that look like the third illustration.

Fold up as described

Glue the two packets together, back to back. When the glue has dried, open up one of the packets, put a 50p piece in its centre, and then close it again. Turn the two packets over and open up the top packet. You are now ready to show your friends how to make money by magic.

Show everyone a 10p coin and place it in the centre of the open sheet. The people watching must not know that you have another packet hidden underneath. Fold the paper up over the ten pence.

Now comes the tricky bit for you must turn the paper packets over without anyone seeing you do it. The easiest way to do this is to transfer the paper purse from hand to hand, simply turning over the packet as you do so, and distracting your audience's attention from your hands by your patter.

When you have secretly turned the packets over you say some suitable magic words and then open up the top packet. Your audience will be surprised to see that the 10p has changed into 50p, by magic.

If someone asks how it is done, offer to sell the magic purse to them for 20p. There is still 10p hidden in the bottom packet but you will have a clear 10p profit.

Distract your audience's
attention from your hands...

MIND
OUT

At Your Service

Some of your local shops may welcome help after school and at weekends. Why not ask them? Much of the work will tend to consist of cleaning up the shop and filling the shelves. If you are lucky you might get the chance to serve the customers.

This type of work is usually advertised in local newspapers or in the window of the shop. But you could also take the first step and approach the shopkeeper yourself.

A good time to apply for shop work is in the weeks before Christmas when shops are particularly busy. In many places, especially in holiday or tourist areas, shops experience an extra demand during the summer and will probably be very pleased for any assistance you can provide.

If you are lucky enough to serve on the counter always remember the old adage "the customer is always right" (even when he or she is wrong!). Shop customers can be very annoying at times but you must always remain courteous.

Remember the old adage...

All Change

If you ever handle cash in your business dealings you should know how to give the right change.

The easiest way is to count upwards at all times.

If, for example, a customer's bill comes to £1.82 and you are given a £5 note you would start from the £1.82 and take change from the till (assuming you are working in a shop) until you reached the £5. Thus, you would remove cash from the till as follows: "£1.82 plus 3p equals £1.85; plus 5p equals £1.90; plus 10p makes £2. And three single pound notes brings the total to £5."

You should hand the change to your customer in the same way, counting up from the £1.82 until you reach £5.

The easiest way is to count upwards at all times

Man (or Woman) About the House

Mind the House

Houseminding is a service you can offer to people who are going on holiday. For an agreed fee, you visit their house at regular intervals during their absence to check that the plants are watered, the fish and the cat are fed (but do not feed the fish to the cat), and that everything is secure.

Make sure you get the key to the house before the people go away.

You should also have a letter from the owner stating that it is all right for you to be on the premises (it could be most embarrassing if the police suspected you of being a burglar).

HOUSE MINDER

Make sure they tell you their holiday address—in case of emergencies.

As an added service, and for an extra fee, you could also offer your talents as a garden-minder—mowing the lawn and generally keeping the garden tidy while they are away (see page 65).

Light housework

There are many jobs you can do for busy housewives. Washing up, making beds, dusting, cleaning silver and brass, hoovering, food preparation, dog-walking, child-minding, etc., etc., etc. You could also offer them a shopping service (see page 38).

You could advertise yourself as being willing to do any light housework. Be careful not to write "lighthouse work" in your advertisement or you may find yourself all at sea.

There are many jobs you can do for busy housewives

Baubles, Bangles, and Beads

Making jewellery is a business that is well worth thinking about if you are good with your hands or you are of an artistic nature.

To make jewellery from stones that you have collected yourself you will need a tumbler. This is not a drinking glass but a machine that grinds and polishes stones. It will cost about £30. If you cannot afford this much then it is possible to buy stones that have been ground and polished ready to be glued into mounts. However, you will make more profit on jewellery made with self-polished stones, and so pay for the cost of the machine within a relatively short time, if you can persuade some kind person to lend you the money.

The design is limited only by your imagination

It is also possible to make extremely attractive jewellery from gold wire. The design of such jewellery is limited only by the extent of your own imagination. No equipment is really necessary for this type of work although a pair of pliers will come in handy. It is also worth having a small table-top vice for doing intricate work.

A pair of pliers will come in handy

A wide range of jewellery can also be made from wood, plastic, and even papier mâché.

One of the nice things about making jewellery is that it is self-advertising. Every time one of your customers wears a piece of jewellery it is seen by a great many other people, all potential customers. With a bit of luck some of these people will ask where the jewellery was made and they may then come to you with an order.

Spot Change

The world famous millionaire Ivor Fortune loves counting his money as you can see in the pictures on this page. He could never take his eyes off his money for long enough to realise that the artist has made ten changes between the two pictures. Can you spot the differences?

Answers on page 128.

How To Make Your Own Gold

If you do not like the idea of having to work to earn some money, you could always try making some gold. All you have to do is to soak some straw in cold water. Keep the straw in the water overnight and then strain the liquid into a china dish. All you now have to do is to leave the liquid at a constant temperature for just one day. At the end of that time there should be a thin skin on the surface of the water. That skin, according to Harry Fell, who patented this recipe in 1884, will be pure gold!

You are welcome to try this method if you like—but it is a pretty sure bet that you will make more money by working for it!

Then strain the liquid into a china dish

Keeping Accounts

If your business is to be run efficiently it is essential that you keep records. Not gramophone records but records of the materials you buy and the items you sell. No matter how small your business venture is at the start, it will prove well worthwhile keeping some form of accounts.

All you need are a few exercise books in which you can write all the necessary information. Use these books to record anything you buy for the business and any money you receive for your efforts. Keep them as neat as you can. If you can't read them they won't be much use.

Your accounts don't have to be very elaborate affairs—just enough for you to see whether or not you are making a profit. If you are in the business of cleaning cars, for example, you

CAR WASH

	Receipts
Polish	
Cloths	
Shampoo (large)	
Dan Druff (2 cars)	1·20
Hal. E. Tosis	·60
Hazel Nutt	·60
Jim Nasium	·60
Polish (large)	
Ben Dover	·60
Joe King	·60
L.E. Fant (2 cars)	1·20
	5·40

PROFIT

will want to know how much you are spending on cloths and polishes—or you may discover that you are not charging enough for your services. Write down the money earned (credit) on a left-hand page, and money spent (debit) on the right-hand page, so you can always quickly tot up your current cash situation. (Another way to do this is to empty out your piggy bank and see what you've got . . .!)

It is also worthwhile analysing the amounts that you spend so you can see which items are costing you a lot of money. You will then be able to take a closer look at these items to see if there is any way of cutting down the cost—for any cost you reduce will result in a similar increase in your profit.

If you do not want anyone else to know how much money you are earning you could keep your accounts in code so that industrial spies will not be able to uncover your secrets.

ACCOUNTS BOOK

Payments
·50
·30
·80

·90

2·50
£2·90 .

NOTE
=
Try keeping your accounts in code

The only code I got is a code in the nose..

Flower Power

Self-raising flowers

One way of earning money from flowers is to grow and sell them. All you need are a few packets of seeds or bulbs and a small patch in the garden. It is often said that money grows on trees but in this instance you could find that money grows on flowers.

Among the many flowers you can easily grow from seed are marigolds (African and French), astors, pansies, and lobelia. Plant the seeds in a shallow, earth-filled box that has been lined with plastic (an old plastic bag will do).

Once the seeds have developed into small shoots you could try selling the plants. Many gardeners will be interested in buying them at this stage and you should get quite a good return for your investment. Any that you do not sell can be further cultivated until they flower and you can then sell the cut flowers.

Many plants develop from bulbs and you can sell these to your customers in bulb form. Such plants include daffodils, lilies, crocuses and snowdrops. There is one type of bulb you cannot develop in this way — a light bulb. You'd have to be really switched on to grow one of them!

All you need is a small patch of garden..

Make your own

Why not try making some flowers? Artificial ones can be made from virtually any material you can think of—paper, cloth, tin, wood, leather, and so on.

An easy way to make artificial flowers is to first obtain two real flowers of the type you wish to make and then to adopt the following procedure:

1. Carefully take one of the flowers to pieces.

Now reassemble the shapes into a complete flower

2. Draw, or trace, the shape of each piece on to a sheet of thick card.

3. Cut out each card shape.

4. Place the shapes on the material you are using and draw around them.

5. Put the card shapes away for future use.

6. Now cut out the material and reassemble the shapes into a complete flower, working from the centre outwards.

7. Depending on the material you are using, you now glue, sew, or wire the pieces together.

8. Do any final shaping that may be required, using the second real flower as a model.

If your flowers are well made then you can sell them at jumble sales, fetes, and to friends.

Drying plants

Some flowers are easier to dry than others. Most flowers, leaves, seed-heads, etc., can be preserved by simply hanging them upside down in a cool place for two to three weeks. Other plants can be preserved by immersing them in a solution of one part glycerine mixed with two parts of warm water. Another method of drying, which often gives better results than the first two, is to immerse the flowers in a box filled with a drying agent called silica gel which is available from most large chemists.

All the flowers and other plants you use should be in good condition and picked on a dry day for best results.

Your dried flowers can be arranged decoratively in vases just like ordinary flowers. An effective way of arranging them is to push them into a styrofoam ball. These balls can be bought in several sizes from florist's shops.

Push a ribbon through the centre of the ball, tie a knot in one end, and then push the flower stems into the ball until it is completely covered with flowers. As the stems tend to be rather brittle, an alternative, and easier, way is to first remove the stems and then glue just the flower heads to the ball. The ribbon is used to hang the flower ball up and it makes an unusual and most attractive decoration.

Jobs You Will Really Dig

There is no shortage of opportunities for good gardeners. There are always a great number of gardening jobs you can do for people. You could mow the lawn, cut the hedge, weed the borders (make sure you know the difference between weeds and flowers), sweep up leaves (*after* they have fallen from the trees), tend bonfires, and a thousand and one other jobs.

Much of the work tends to be seasonal, and you may be restricted by the weather at times. But if you like the outdoor life and enjoy gardening this could be just the job for you.

Much of the work tends to be seasonal.

Empty houses
Surprising as it may seem, you may also get gardening jobs at empty houses. If there is a "For Sale" notice up, approach the estate agents and offer to keep the garden tidy until someone buys the property. This could be to the agent's advantage, for he is more likely to sell the property if the garden is neat and tidy.

Offer to do the same for other houses on his books, provide the same service to other estate agents, and you could soon have a lot of work to do.

If the agent is not interested, keep an eye on the property anyway. As soon as someone moves in, offer to tidy up the garden for them. The new house owner will probably have enough to think about and may be very pleased to have this chore taken off his hands.

keep an eye on the property anyway...

Grow and sell

If you like growing things but do not like the idea of looking after other people's gardens you could grow plants and vegetables for sale.

All you need for plants is a supply of pots, some potting compost, and some seeds.

If you intend to grow vegetables you may have to persuade your dad to let you use part of the garden.

As a variation you could even try growing some unusual plants from carrot tops, peach stones, fruit pips, and so on.

POTS OF MONEY

Coin Turnover

Three new coins have recently been issued by the Bank of Upper Umboto. The top row of pictures on this page shows the "heads" side of the coins and the bottom row shows the "tails". The coins in the two rows are not, however, in the same positions. If the eagle is not on the same coin as the snake what creature is on the reverse of the lion?

Answer on page 128.

There's No Business Like Show Business

If you can sing, dance, tell jokes, do impressions, juggle, or put on a puppet show then you could make money as an entertainer. It can be difficult for young people, to start with, because people tend to assume that you will be prepared to demonstrate your skills for nothing. But make it clear you expect to be paid and you will eventually win through.

To be a good entertainer you must have a good act. Try to perfect everything you do up to professional standards—or as near as you can make it. When you have devised your act and rehearsed it thoroughly you can offer your services for parties, fetes, and other occasions.

At first you may have to advertise in your local newspaper but after a while you will find that "word of mouth" is the best publicity of all. People who have liked your performance will tell their friends and, hopefully, they will then book you for their next event.

If you are really good perhaps one day you will earn as much as the American singer Liza Minelli, who once received £40,000 for an appearance in a New Year's Eve show at a club in New York.

Tour de Force

Working as a local guide is a really fascinating job if you have an interest in the area in which you live. You will have to do a lot of research, but a great deal of useful information can be obtained from your local library and the nearest tourist information office.

Work out some interesting tours of your area. It is a good idea to devise several tours, each dealing with a specific topic. You could, for example, have a tour of local buildings that have architectural or historical significance. Other tours could be of local churches, statues in the town, companies, or farms. Always ask permission from anyone concerned.

Have a set speech prepared for each aspect of your tour. Although rehearsed this must appear to be spontaneous— and it must, of course, be interesting! In addition to your prepared patter you must also be ready to answer a variety of questions. To be a good guide you also have to be a walking, talking encyclopedia!

To start off as a guide in your area, advise the local tourist office, the local chamber of commerce, local hotels, and travel agents of your intentions. Local bus companies and taxi services should also be told of the fact that you are prepared to guide visitors to the area.

If you live in an out-of-the-way place, you may not get much call for your services. But if you are at a seaside resort, a place of historical interest, or a place that attracts a lot of visitors for some other reason you could easily be rushed off your feet.

If you live in an out-of-the -way place, you may not get too much call on your services

69

Be a Jack of All Trades
(or How to Become Stinking Rich)

If you set up business as a Jack (or Jill) of all Trades, doing all manner of odd jobs, you must be prepared to do dirty work on many occasions. You must be prepared to accept jobs such as cleaning out chicken coops, mucking out stables, degreasing engines, clearing attics, or shovelling manure.

You could even specialise in doing dirty jobs—but you will need a pair of overalls to keep your clothes clean. It is also worth buying a tin of barrier cream. This is to put on your hands before starting a job and makes it a great deal easier to wash your hands clean afterwards (assuming, of course, that you do wash occasionally).

The problem with doing a wide range of jobs is fixing a fair price for each job. Possibly the best way is to decide upon an hourly rate which will make it worth your while for both the clean and easy work as well as the hard and dirty jobs.

If your customer agrees to an hourly rate it does not mean you should work slowly in order to receive more money. Your customers will soon cotton on to that dodge and the news that you are lazy will soon get around.

Work hard, give value for money, don't be frightened of dirty work, and people will soon ask you to do jobs for them.

Making Money from Nothing

If you think it is necessary to actually do something to make money you could be wrong. There are several examples of people who have made money from absolutely nothing.

A London canning company once produced sealed empty cans and sold them as tins of "bracing sea air".

The Nothing Book was a best seller in America. Described as "the ideal bedside companion for the heavy sleeper" it consisted of 160 blank pages—just the book for people who can't read!

For nine years actress Jane Comfort was paid to do nothing. She was understudy for the role of Mrs Boyle in the play *The Mousetrap* but had to take the part only twice. For the rest of the time she sat in her dressing-room, knitting.

In Toronto, Canada a store offered "topless and bottomless bathing suits". At least a hundred women queued to receive their box of absolutely nothing. Whether or not those ladies actually wore their "bathing suits" has not been recorded.

An art dealer in Papillion, Nebraska, USA, received over two hundred dollars when he advertised in his local newspaper. He offered "absolutely nothing" for one dollar—and received 235 orders!

A Safe Place for Your Money

One of the big secrets of becoming rich is to live as cheaply as you can and to save as much money as possible. Saving some of your hard-earned cash is a habit you should try to develop as quickly as you can.

Decide how much you need to spend each week and then stick to that amount. Put the rest into savings and you will be surprised how quickly it mounts up. There are many ways of saving and you would be well advised to look at some of them before deciding where to keep your money.

You could put it under your mattress or in a piggy bank. This may be fine for very small amounts but if you really want to save properly you should put your money where it will earn some more money. This is usually done by putting it into a bank, a building society or the Post Office. You are in effect lending them the money and they will then pay you for this privilege. The money they pay you is called "interest" (see page 76). It is very satisfying to realise that you are making money without doing anything for it.

If you do not earn enough money to have to pay income tax the amount of interest you make will probably be highest in a bank deposit account. A building society account will pay less interest but in the long term could be a much worthwhile investment if you hope to buy your own house one day. Building societies lend people money to buy houses and they are much more inclined to give a mortgage (a loan to buy a house) to people who have been regular savers with them over a period of time.

If you get to the stage where you have several hundred pounds in savings, then there are other means, (such as loans to local authorities) of making higher rates of interest. Usually with such methods you have to agree to lend the money for a predetermined period of perhaps five years or even longer. If you decide you want your money back before that time is up you will lose your interest.

One thing to remember with all forms of savings is to try not to spend the interest you have earned, for if this is left in the account it too will earn interest and your money will begin to grow quite appreciably over the years.

It is possible for someone under eighteen to buy stocks and shares which, in effect, means that you are buying part of a large company. If the company makes money the value of your shares will go up. Apart from the fact that you have to convince a stockbroker (a man who buys and sells stocks and shares) that you have sufficient money to cover the cost, as any contract cannot be legally enforced until you are eighteen, stocks and shares are not recommended as a form of investment for the young tycoon. There is no guarantee that you will make any money—in fact you are more likely to lose some or even all of it. Far better to put your money into a bank or a building society.

The Post Office
At the Post Office you can open a National Savings Account. There are two types of account—ordinary and investment. You have to be over seven to have either of these accounts. Money can be deposited or withdrawn at any post office and interest is paid on the money you keep in your account. The investment account carries a higher rate of interest than an ordinary account but you have to give a month's notice if you wish to take out any money.

The National Savings Organisation also issues National Savings Certificates which provide a good rate of interest but you have to leave your money in them for a specified period of years.

Banks

To open a bank account you have to be over seven years of age. There are two types of account—deposit and current. A deposit account is a form of savings account and the bank will pay interest on money in the account. You can withdraw money from this account but you will lose some interest if you do not give the bank a week's notice of the proposed withdrawal.

Banks do not pay interest on current accounts. It is this type of account for which cheque books are issued so customers can pay their bills easily. As a general rule the bank will not issue a cheque book to someone under sixteen, although there have been exceptions. It is easy to bank money or withdraw money from this account just by going into the bank and completing a small slip.

Some banks require that you keep a certain amount in your current account or they will charge you for it. Others do not make charges for young people, so check before you open an account.

Building Societies

If you are old enough to sign your name, then you are old enough to open an account with a building society. To open the account you will have to pay in a small amount—usually about £1—and that will have to remain in the account to keep it active. After that you can pay in how much you want whenever you want. And provided that you have enough money in your account, you can draw out money as well.

The big disadvantage of running a building society account is that income tax is deducted from the interest you receive. This happens even though you may not be eligible to pay income tax in normal circumstances.

Before deciding what type of account is best for your savings have a word with your parents and your teachers—and have a look around for yourself.

One of your best bets, if you are earning a reasonable amount from your business, would probably be to open a bank current account and a building society or national savings account. You then instruct your bank to pay a fixed amount each month into your savings account. This monthly payment should be as high as you can make it without putting too much of a strain on your resources.

When you do eventually get yourself an account, keep a check on the figures. Although the accounts are all controlled by computers, some mistakes do slip through. Apart from this it is still worth keeping a regular check on your money so you know exactly your money position at all times.

BANK ACCOUNT 3/1
BUILDING SOC. 8/2
NAT SAVINGS 10/1
STOCK MARKET 15/1
RAFFLES 20/1
BINGO 50/1
IRISH SWEEP 500/1

A Matter of Interest

If you put money into savings you should expect it to earn some interest. If you borrow money you will expect to pay interest on the amount you borrow. Interest is the amount paid by a borrower to a lender for the use of the money.

There are two forms of interest: simple and compound.

Simple interest is a set amount paid, usually expressed as a percentage (an amount for each hundred pounds) of the amount borrowed, no matter how long the period of the loan.

Thus, if you borrowed £100 at 10% (ten per cent) interest per annum (a posh way of saying 'each year') you would pay £10 a year until you paid back the principal (the amount borrowed).

So, if you lend someone £100 at 10% simple interest for five years your total amount in five years time would be £150.

If you were to invest £280 over a period of eight years at 7½% the amount of interest you will receive will be £168. Adding that to the original amount of £280 makes a total of £448 at the end of the eight years. That's not bad is it!

But compound interest proves to be an even better deal for the lender. In compound interest the amount of interest is added to the original amount and the total attained is used to calculate the interest for the following period. In other words you receive interest on the interest. Sounds interesting doesn't it?

So, going back to the original example of £100 invested for five years at 10% the total amount of interest received over the period would be £61.05. This is a slight increase on the £50 earned using simple interest but over longer period (and with higher amounts) the difference is even more marked.

With the second example of £280 invested for a period of eight years at 7½% you would receive interest of £219.39 over the period compared with £168 using simple interest.

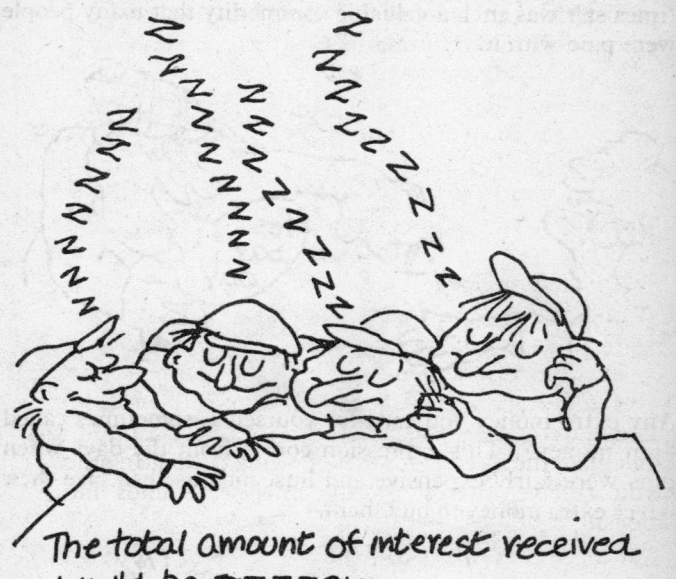

The total amount of interest received would be zzzzero

In these examples the amount of odd pence has been included in the calculations but in actual practice banks and building societies calculate interest only on whole pounds.

So, if anyone now asks you why you put money into a building society you can always say: "I do it as a matter of interest".

Money Talk

Our word "money" comes from ancient Rome where a mint was established in a building once used as a temple to the goddess Moneta. It is from this that our words like money, monetary and mint have derived.

The word "salary" comes from "salt" because in ancient times salt was such a valuable commodity that many people were paid with it.

Any extra money you earn for yourself is sometimes called "pin money". This expression comes from the days when pins were fairly expensive and husbands used to give their wives extra money to buy them.

If you pay your bills promptly it may be said that you have "paid on the nail". In British markets there used to be pillars, called "nails". These were used by merchants as counters on which to place their cash when paying money to someone else. It is from the use of these "nails" that the expression originates.

Unemployed people in the British Isles are entitled to receive money from the State. This is commonly referred to as the "dole", a word that originated with the Old English word "dal", meaning a portion. The word "dole" was first used to describe that set portion of money or food given to the poor by charitable organisations.

The slang word "bread" for "money" comes from cockney rhyming slang where money was described as "bread and honey".

The word "tip", meaning a gratuity, comes from the initials of the words "To Insure Promptness".

When something is very cheap it is often said that it is "going for a song". It is believed that this expression arose either from the cheap song sheets that were sold in days gone by or from the small change given to buskers who sang outside inns.

In American slang the word "buck" means a dollar. The word comes from the days when trappers were paid fifty cents for a doe's skin and twice as much (one dollar) for the skin of a buck.

Someone who is born into a rich family is said to have been "born with a silver spoon in his mouth". This expression comes from the practice of wealthy godparents presenting a silver spoon to a child at its christening.

Our word "bankrupt" comes from the Italian words "banca" (bench) and "rupt" (broken). In Venice during the Middle Ages bankers carried on their business in the marketplace seated at wooden benches. Any banker who could not settle his debts was banned from the market place and his bench was broken up. Nowadays any businessman who is unable to pay his debts is said to be "bankrupt".

Any banker who could not pay his debts had his bench broken up.

Have You Got Change For an Aspirin?

Many unusual things have been used for money through the years. Blocks of salt were once used, for salt was a valuable commodity in times past. Other things used for money include tea in Russia and cowrie shells in the Pacific Islands. The North American Indians used beads or shells for their currency. In other parts of North America dried fish, tobacco, and even fish hooks have been used for money.

On the island of Yap in the Pacific, enormous stones formed the currency. Some of the stones were so large that they could not be lifted and had to be left on the ground, but everyone   on the island knew to whom each large stone belonged so the system worked extremely well. The stones came from the Pelew Islands some two hundred miles away and as no similar stones were found naturally on Yap they had a rarity value that made them ideal material for currency.

From May 1841 to May 1842 the money used in Mexico and Texas consisted of bars of soap! Each bar was stamped with the name of the town in which it could be used but in some areas there were local agreements where towns would accept the soap used by other towns nearby. Unfortunately some people lost money as a result of this strange currency for once the official stamp wore off, the soap was of no use— except for washing!

This town's all washed up pardner.

For some eighty years the French colonists in Canada used playing cards as money. They proved an acceptable currency because everyone believed the French government would eventually redeem them in gold or silver. But when the English took control of Canada in 1763 the French refused to honour the debt. In order to calm the settlers the British offered to pay holders of this "Monnaie de Carte", as it was known, a quarter of its face value.

And these strange forms of money do not belong only to the past. In 1973 there was a shortage of small coins in Portugal. This resulted in people using sweets or stamps as currency for a while. Aspirins were once used as money in San Luis, Argentina and a similar thing happened in Mexico City when a number of one centavo pieces made a mysterious disappearance. There was not time to mint a replacement supply so small pieces of chewing gum were used instead—no doubt the gum was mint flavour.

Designs on Money

This is the design for a new note to be issued by the Bank of Looschange. Unfortunately the artist tore a piece out of it by mistake. Can you decide which of the pieces shown below fits the hole?

Answers on page 128.

The Art of Car Washing

Car washing is a popular way of earning extra money. To be successful, however, you should realise that there is quite an art to washing a car properly, so do read through the following points thoroughly before starting work.

Car washing can be a damp and sometimes mucky job, so don't wear your Sunday best clothes. It is worthwhile investing in a pair of rubber gloves. They will protect your hands and keep them clean.

You will find that the job is much easier when there are two or more people to do it. If you decide to work with others, make sure that everyone is agreed, before you start on how the profits are to be divided. It may prove a good idea for one of you to keep a simple account book in which to record everything you receive and everything you spend so there can be no arguments later.

Draw up a scale of charges and explain them to your customers before you start. It would be quite fair to charge more for a larger car than you would for a Mini. The customer should also be prepared to pay if you use a shampoo on the car and more still if he wants it polished as well. Use your accounts book to record the cost of shampoos and polishes. If they go up in price you should adjust your prices accordingly.

It's worthwhile to invest in a pair of rubber gloves

If the customer has a hose you will get much better results than with just buckets of water. Running the hose over the car will help to get the dirt off. But be careful where you point it. If you direct it straight on to the side windows it will eventually seep through the rubber and corrode the insides of the doors. The rubber surrounds of the side windows were not designed to withstand a direct flow of water. Be careful not to point the hose straight down either. You will end up with your wellies full of water.

The rubber surrounds to the side windows are not designed to withstand a direct flow of water

Start with the top of the car. (See page 87 for a handy tool to reach right across the roof.) This is the cleanest part but the water will also help to loosen the dirt on the sides, the boot, and the bonnet where the dirt is much thicker.

When you have finished the roof go on to the bonnet, then the boot, and then the sides. Always remember to use plenty of water and to rinse the car well.

Never rub hard when washing a car as this will cause any grit on the car to scratch the bodywork. If there are stubborn areas of dirt use more water.

Use a separate cloth, preferably a clean chamois leather,

for the windows. It is a good idea to put a drop of methylated spirit in with the water used on windows.

The dirtiest areas of the car will be around the wheels. Use a separate cloth or stiff brush for these areas. Make sure you wash underneath the wheel arches, preferably with a hose at high pressure. This is usually the dirtiest part of the car and the owner will appreciate the fact that you have done your job properly.

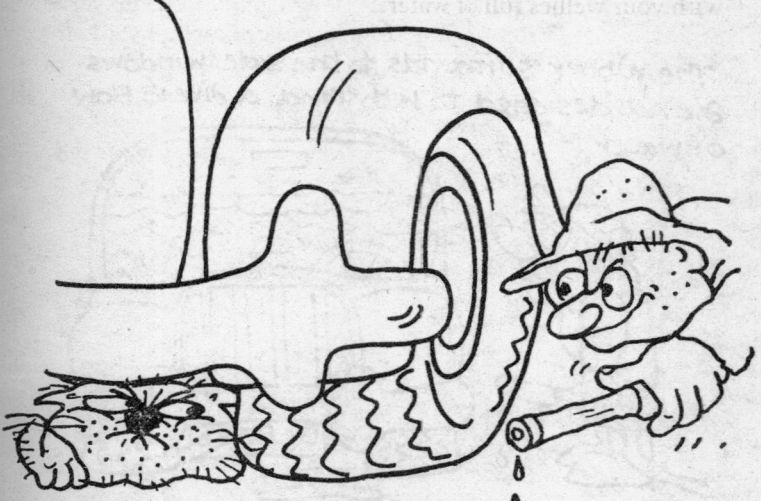

The dirtiest areas of the car will be around the wheels

Now give the car a good rinse, either by playing the hose all over it or by chucking buckets of water at it. Then use a soft cloth or a leather to dry the car off, ready for polishing. Alternatively you could use a shampoo that has a built-in wax protection. This will save the need for polishing and yet provide the car with a nice shine.

Collect your money (you've earned it) and get ready to start on the next one!

Reaching for the Top

One of the problems when washing cars is being able to reach across the windscreen, and across the roof. Here are a couple of simple devices you can make to enable you to cover these areas without any difficulty.

The first, for windscreens, is simply an old car windscreen wiper attached to a pole. The wiper can be bought from a motor accessory shop or you may be able to pick one up very cheaply, or even for nothing, from a garage or a junkyard. If you use an old one, buy a new rubber wiper blade for it so it works more effectively.

Attach the wiper to a long pole with string or wire. You can now reach across the windscreen quite easily, wiping off the water and dirt with your patent wiper.

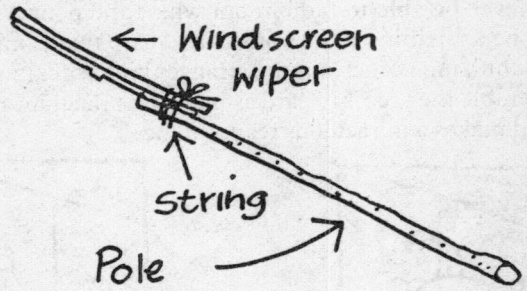

The second device works on the same principle and is simply a brush tied to a pole by its handle. This will enable you to reach the top of the car. You can use it for the windscreen as well but make sure the brush is a soft one and that you use plenty of water.

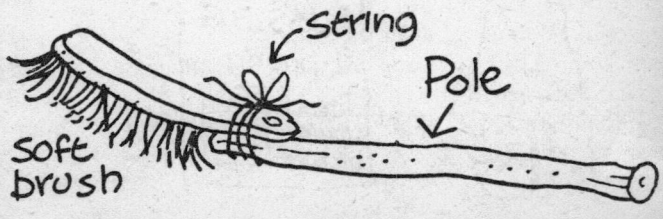

The Disappearing Pound

Trace the picture shown on the opposite page on to a sheet of thin card. As the copy must be exact you may find it easier to get the page photocopied and then glue it on to the card. Cut the card into pieces as shown by the dotted lines.

Now put the card together as it was originally and count the number of pound signs you can see. There are actually 56 but please check for yourself.

Imagine that the pieces are marked as in the first of the small diagrams. Move the pieces apart and then reassemble them as in the second diagram.

Now count the pound signs again you will find that one has mysteriously disappeared.

You can show this amazing card to your friends but they will never be able to fathom out where the pound went. It must be something to do with that square that is missing in the right hand corner but the strange thing is that when you reassemble the pieces of card as in the first diagram again the pound makes a miraculous reappearance!

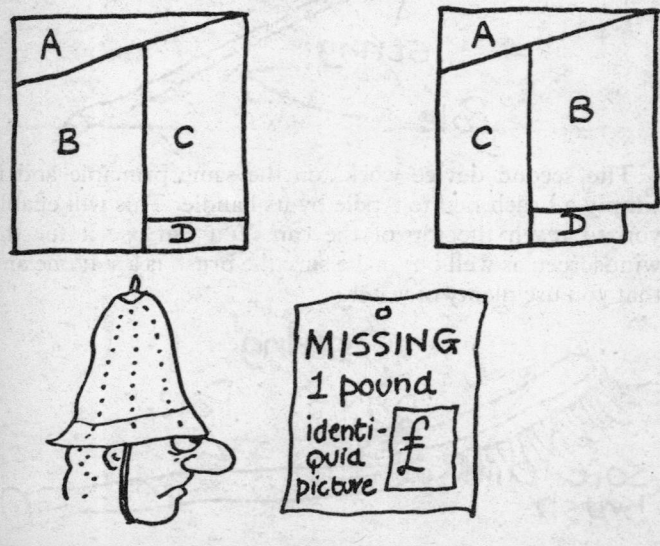

World Currencies

Once you become a millionaire it is very likely that you will be conducting business deals in many parts of the world. To do this you will need to know something about the currencies used worldwide. Test your knowledge with this quiz. Can you say in which country you would expect to find each of the different types of money listed below?

LIRE
ZLOTY
GUILDER
DRACHMA
KRONE
DEUTSCHEMARK
YUAN
ROUBLE
SCHILLING
YEN
KYAT
BOLIVAR

Answers on page 128.

Animal Antics

If you like animals, here are a few jobs you can try:

Pet minding
This job is rather like babysitting but you look after animals instead of children. As a lot of children behave like animals you should not find there is too much of a difference!

Your pet minding service can be offered to people who are out for the day, away for the weekend, or off on holiday (provided of course that they have a pet). In most cases you will be asked to look after the pets in your own home so make sure your mother knows—she may not take too kindly to having a crocodile in the bath! In view of this it could be a good idea to restrict this type of service to smaller animals!

Dog walking
Walking dogs for friends and neighbours will not only earn you money, it will also give you some exercise. Until you get to know the dogs only take one out at a time. Eventually you may be able to take out two, three, or even four—but make sure they are friendly or you could have a fight on your hands!

Breeding pets

Money can be made by breeding animals but care has to be taken in selecting which animal to breed. This will be determined by whether or not there is a market for the animal, the space you have available, the amount of time you can spare, and whether or not your parents approve.

To start with you would be advised to restrict your interests to small animals such as rabbits, mice, hampsters, small birds, fish, or cats. When you have gained some experience then perhaps you can move on to bigger and better things such as elephants, boa constrictors, or gorillas!

Care has to be taken in selecting which animal to breed

Winning Ways

You might think that entering competitions is not a good way of earning money because of the element of chance involved. But entering competitions can be conducted just like any other business. And with a little thought it is possible to increase your chances of winning.

There are literally hundreds of competitions from which you can choose. Someone wins the prizes—there is no reason why it should not be you.

Rules

The most important thing to do is to read the rules. It sounds obvious but it is a fact that many competition entries are disqualified because the entrant did not read the rules properly.

Facts

Many competitions set a series of factual questions. If you have a good encyclopedia, access to a library, or you are a genius, the answers to these should cause no problems.

Slogans

Some competitions also require that you invent a witty slogan or complete a sentence in less than ten words saying why you always eat Kloggs Krunchy Korn Kakes, or whatever. It is the slogan that will win or lose you the competition (assuming you have answered the questions correctly) so it is worth spending some time on it. The following tips should help:

1. Do not put down the first thing that comes into your head. Give it some thought.
2. Write down every idea you can think of then put down the best.
3. Use a slogan that incorporates a clever use of words.
4. Slogans that rhyme also stand a good chance of winning.
5. It is worthwhile having a thesaurus (a book that lists words of similar meaning) and a good dictionary to hand.

The business of competitions

As a business, entering competitions is not a reliable source of income. But it can be a great deal of fun. Just remember one thing—there is only one type of person that wins competitions and that is the person that enters competitions.

And the more competitions you enter the more chance you have of winning something you have always wanted—like a year's supply of gerbil food, a ton of tin tacks, a herd of elephants, or a term of imprisonment on Devil's Island!

Fishy Business

Angling for cash

This is a job that really has a catch in it but in this case it is a catch that could make you some useful money.

If you are a keen and successful fisherman (or fisherwoman) you can make money by selling the fish you catch. Your neighbours and friends will usually be pleased to buy them provided you charge a reasonable price.

Take a look in your local fishmonger's shop to find out the cost of the type of fish you catch. This will give you an idea of what the fish is worth but make your price much lower than the fishmonger's. You could even have a word with your fishmonger. He may be prepared to buy your fish from you if you can guarantee a more or less regular supply.

Breeding bait

If you know a number of anglers you should make money breeding maggots for bait. But check with your mother first—she may not like the thought of hundreds of live maggots inhabiting the garden shed!

£ for lures

It is amazing how much keen fishermen are prepared to pay for the flies, or lures, they use. Making them is not easy but if you have patience and skillful fingers it could prove a rewarding and relaxing job.

In theory no special equipment is required, but the job is much easier if you are prepared to invest in some basic items—a small vice, a pair of scissors, a bobbin holder, a dubbing needle, and some hackle pliers. All of these items will be available from a fishing tackle shop. You will also need a whip tool (not for whipping but to tie thread more easily than doing it by hand).

The materials required will vary according to the type and variety of flies you make but should include feathers of various types, gossamer thread, varnish, hooks, and some fly tying wax (beeswax).

If you learn to make flies really well you may one day do as well as Jackie Wakeford. When she left school at 16 she began selling flies to local fishermen. She did so well that she opened a small shop at the back of her parents' house. Although she is now married with a young daughter she continues to sell flies to fishermen by mail order. So great was Jackie's success that in 1981 she published a book, *Fly-Tying Techniques*, describing how to make flies. If you wish to go into the fly business success it could be well worth your while getting hold of a copy.

In Your Own Write

If you have a love of words, reasonably good English, and something interesting or original to say perhaps you could build up a business as a writer.

At first you could try writing for your school magazine. If you do not have a school magazine why not start one? You could then perhaps begin to submit articles or stories to your local newspaper.

First study the magazine or newspaper for which you wish to write. You will then get to know the type of material it publishes and the style in which it is written.

Your submission should be typed in double spacing on A4 paper and the whole thing should convey a neat, well-organised appearance.

With your article you should enclose a stamped addressed envelope for its return if it is not wanted—and don't forget to keep a record of the postage, it can mount up quite quickly.

Do not worry too much if your masterpiece is rejected. All writers receive rejection slips. Try to work out why the item has been rejected. Most editors are too busy to tell you the reason—you have to work it out for yourself.

Keep It on File

The thought of setting up a filing system is enough to make almost any businessman go pale. And yet filing is really quite simple. All it means is keeping paper in a certain order so you can find them again when you need them.

There is no need to buy expensive files and equipment for your filing system. Every potential millionaire should realise the importance of saving as much money as possible, so if you need a filing system why not make your own?

All you will need is a number of envelopes all the same shape and size. If you can find someone who has a number of used envelopes they will probably cost you nothing at all. Mark each envelope with a letter of the alphabet or some other indication of what papers are to be kept in it. Put the envelopes in order and keep them in a large cardboard box obtained from your local supermarket. You could cover the box with coloured paper to make it look smarter but this is not really necessary.

Any papers or notes about a particular subject are simply dropped into the appropriate envelope. Because the envelopes are kept in order you will always be able to find something when you want it.

Try and find someone who has a number of used envelopes

Giving it Away

Some people appear to have so much money that they are willing to give it away to whoever will take it. That is not always so easy as it would seem, however. In 1973 Walter Harrington tried to give away £300 in Glastonbury. He handed the money to passers-by in celebration of the fact that he had just been offered a job—but people became suspicious and contacted the police.

Many of the people to whom he offered money refused it, thinking it was some sort of trick. Others refused thinking it was a publicity stunt, and many believed the money to have been stolen. But the money was his and the offers were genuine. All he was trying to do was to bring a little happiness into other people's lives.

In 1975 readers of the *Reading Chronicle* were surprised to find a £1 note tucked into their newspaper. People telephoned the editor to thank him but he knew nothing about it! Others rang the newsagent to ask if he had mislaid the money but he knew nothing about it either. Both men and the people who received the £1 notes were completely mystified by the occurrence.

A few months later a man was seen showering £10 notes from a lorry on to bewildered motorists. Afterwards he went to the police and requested his money back. The reason for his strange act? He had apparently offered £500 to his girlfriend as a gift but she had refused to accept it so he decided to give it away. And then he changed his mind!

Luckily for that man the majority of the British public are very honest and most of the money was handed in. The same thing happened when money was thrown from a car on the main London to Brighton road in June, 1971. It had been flung out of the window by a two year-old girl. Her father, Peter Calvert, who was taking the money to the bank, did not realise what his daughter was doing until it was too late!

Some people are prepared to give away large sums of money in the form of tips for services rendered. One of the biggest tips on record was that made by William Cunningham of Glasgow in 1930 when he tipped a French barman £3,200. And yet most people say that Scotsmen are mean! Mind you, he did have a reason. He had just won £28,000 in the local casino.

Some other large tippers have tipped highly by accident. One such person was the famous golfer Lee Trevino. When he visited a casino in Southport, Lancashire, in 1968, he gave out several £10 tips to the staff. This was due to the fact that he was unfamiliar with British currency. He thought he was giving away ten shillings (50p) notes.

Some Unusual Cheques

Although it is usual for a cheque to be made out on the special form supplied by a bank, it is quite legal for it to be made out on almost anything. Cheques have in fact been written on cows, dinner plates, and even on people, and they have still proved acceptable to the bank on which they were drawn.

An RAF Officer once wrote a cheque on a biscuit—it is just as well that no-one ate it!

Cheques have even been written on people

Usually these unusual cheques are made out as some form of protest—like that drawn by the Buckingham councillor who paid his rates with a cheque drawn on a paving slab. It took two people to carry the cheque to the local council offices but presumably succeeded in getting the councillor's message across that the local pavements were in a disgusting state.

A similar protest was made by a West Country newsagent who paid his annual rates bill with a cheque written on a 200lb block of concrete shaped like a tombstone.

Maureen Venn of Tandridge in Surrey also protested about her rates. She drew her cheque on a pair of children's panties. Perhaps that was the origin of the slang expression for 50p being "half a knicker".

Builder Chris Wainwright of Bromsgrove in Kent paid part of a fine imposed on him by local magistrates with a cheque written on a toilet! No doubt the magistrates paid it into the bank at their convenience.

An American income tax office once received a cheque written on another form of clothing. The irate man who sent the cheque to the tax inspectors told them: "Now you have got everything." The cheque was written on one of his shirts.

Money in the Mattress

In spite of the fact that we talk a great deal about money (or the lack of it), many people have the wrong idea about looking after it. It is an old joke that a lot of people keep their money in the mattress—but it's true. Many people do keep their money in a mattress—and a lot end up losing their life savings as a result.

A lady in Doncaster once bought an old mattress for 50p in a jumble sale. She gave it to her children to play on but after a while the mattress split—and out fell £500 in pound notes! Although the lady declared her find to the police, the rightful owner was never found.

Another mattress hoard was found in America a few years ago when a company received an old mattress for re-stuffing. They removed the old stuffing and found it consisted of money—over £10,000 in all!

But mattresses are not the only things in which people keep money. A great number of people keep their cash in even more unusual places.

In Nottinghamshire the organisers of a piano wrecking contest almost destroyed over three hundred pounds when they collected an old piano from a house. They had not gone very far when a man came racing after them, opened the lid, and grabbed the money. His mother had given the piano away without knowing that was where her son kept his savings!

A young lady in London used to keep her savings in an old envelope. Her mother was tidying up one day and she threw the envelope into the dustbin. By the time the girl discovered what her mother had done the dustbin had been collected and all the rubbish taken to the local rubbish dump.

The girl and her mother contacted the local cleansing inspector who told them that the valuable envelope could be anywhere in a pile of five tons of rubbish. But as there was £140 in the envelope it was agreed that it would be worth searching for. "Searching for a needle in a haystack has got nothing on this" remarked the inspector as they sifted through old bottles, tea bags, rotting food, paper, and everything else that had been collected from all the dustbins in the area. They searched all the way through the rubbish but the envelope was nowhere to be seen. They then decided to split the rubbish into smaller piles and to go through each pile separately. After two hours searching one of the men found the crumpled envelope. The girl hugged the man and wept tears of joy for she had been saving the money for her honeymoon.

A gentleman in Wrexham was not so lucky. He hid £500 in some old clothing and his wife threw the clothes into the dustbin. He rushed to the local rubbish dump but searched in vain. Even a mechanical digger he hired failed to find the missing money.

The moral of all these tales is that you should keep your money in a safe place, such as a bank—provided that the bank is not robbed!

What Do I Do Next?

When you become a busy business person you will find there are times when you have so many things to do you cannot decide which is the most important. Some people simply toss a coin to decide what to do next but that is not very scientific. The system described here is a little more reliable and it will help you to put all your jobs in order of priority. At first sight it looks rather complicated but if you follow it through you will find it is much easier than it looks—and, what is more, it works!

Let us assume that you have ten jobs to do. First write them down and letter them A to J like this:

A. Do my accounts
B. Wash the dog
C. Write to Jim Fishface
D. Dig the garden for treasure
E. Feed the cat
F. Buy some sweets
G. Make a customer file
H. Read the Whizzkid's Handbook
I. Make a book rack
J. Write out an advertising card

Because there are so many jobs it is difficult to compare one with another to get an idea of each one's importance and urgency. But it can be done—this is how you do it.

First write down the letter A one less times than the number of jobs there are. In this case there are ten jobs so you write down the letter A nine times. Beneath each letter put the other letters for your jobs.

```
A  A  A  A  A  A  A  A  A
B  C  D  E  F  G  H  I  J
```

Underneath that write the letter B eight times and put the remaining letters underneath. Do the same with C (seven times), D (six times), E (five times), and so on through the letters until you get to I which is written down only once.

You should now have a grid of letters that looks like this:

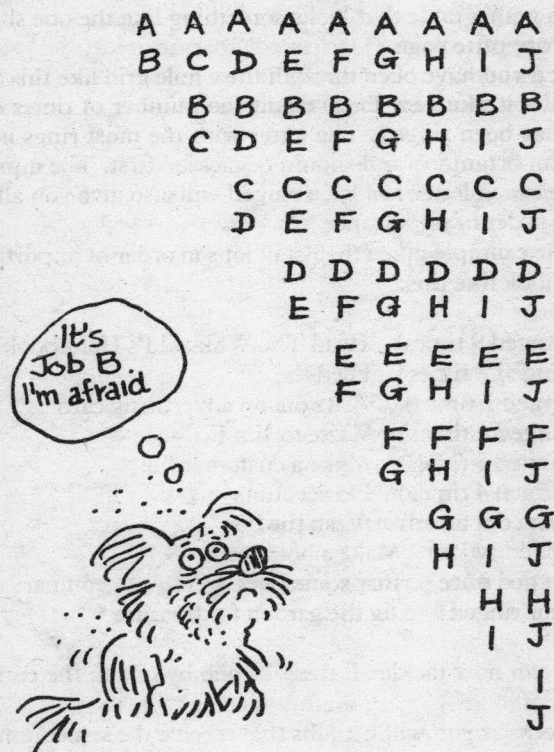

It's Job B I'm afraid

```
A A A A A A A A A A
B C D E F G H I J
    B B B B B B B B
    C D E F G H I J
        C C C C C C C
        D E F G H I J
            D D D D D D
            E F G H I J
                E E E E E
                F G H I J
                    F F F F
                    G H I J
                        G G G
                        H I J
                            H H
                            I J
                                I
                                J
```

Now go along the first line looking at each pair of letters. At the first pair (A/B) you decide whether or not job A is more important or urgent than job B. For a businessman it is more than likely that job A (doing the accounts) is more important than job B (wash the dog)—so put a pencil ring around letter A. Do the same with the next two letters—is job A more important than job C? Put a ring around the letter which is the most important.

When you have gone all the way along the row you will have compared job A with every other job you have to do. Do the same with the second and subsequent rows and you will end up with a table that looks something like the one shown on the opposite page.

When you have been through the whole grid like this (and it does not take very long) count the number of times each letter has been ringed. The letter with the most rings is the most important job and should be tackled first. The number of times each letter has been ringed will also give you all ten jobs in order of importance.

In the example given the list of jobs in order of importance would look like this:

H (ringed 9 times)   Read The Whizzkid's Handbook
E (ringed 8 times)   Feed the cat
J (ringed 7 times)   Write out an advertising card
C (ringed 6 times)   Write to Jim Fishface
G (ringed 5 times)   Make a customer file
A (ringed 4 times)   Do accounts
B (ringed 3 times)   Wash the dog
I (ringed twice)   Make a book rack
F (ringed once)   Buy some sweets
D (not ringed)   Dig the garden for treasure

You can now tackle all the jobs one by one in the correct order.

Sometimes you will get jobs that receive the same number of rings. When this occurs you simply compare the two jobs, decide which of the two is more important, and put that one down first.

A = 4
B = 3
C = 6
D = 0
E = 8
F = 1
G = 5
H = 9
I = 2
J = 7

Digging Up a Fortune

It is not the most reliable of professions, but treasure-hunting can bring in some appreciable gains for anyone who is prepared to take it seriously. Although it is not absolutely essential to have any equipment it will not be long before you decide to buy a metal detector. These range in price from about £12 to several hundred pounds.

Possibly the most important aspect of treasure-hunting is knowing where to look in the first place. Towpaths, footpaths, old fairground sites, commons, market areas, and anywhere else that people gathered in the past are all good places to look.

Old rubbish tips are another useful source of material, particularly bottles and crockery. To find old rubbish tips in your area consult old maps of the region, ask at your library, and inquire at the local council offices.

Consult your library

Much of what you find (particularly from rubbish tips) may appear to have no value at first sight. Old bottles and broken clay pipes do not sound very exciting—except to a collector, for people do collect such items and they may be willing to buy them from you.

If you live in a house that is more than fifty years old you

have a good chance of finding something interesting. Take a look in the attic, the cellar, and the garden. It will also be worth while looking under the floorboards but it is best to get your father's permission before you start pulling them up!

The river banks of tidal rivers are possibly the best and most reliable source of good finds. The water is continually wearing away at the banks perhaps to reveal items that may have been buried for hundreds of years. The best part of the river in which to go treasure hunting is either on a bend or at the mouth but make sure you know what time the tide comes in or you could get caught.

It has been estimated that over 150,000,000 coins disappear from circulation each year in Britain. With a metal detector you have a good chance of finding some of these. In fact, it has been said that a sensible treasure-hunter could find at least 20,000 coins in a year. Even if they are all ½p pieces you will have found £100 which covers the cost of most metal detectors—and from then on the rest is pure profit.

Many of the coins that disappear, along with jewellery and other small items, are lost on beaches. It is therefore no wonder that beach-combing (no, you do not need a comb to do it) has proved a lucrative occupation for many people. If you go beach-combing, first take note of where holiday-makers normally congregate. These are the areas in which you stand a better chance of finding something—usually lots of bottle tops!

Before you go treasure-hunting, though, make sure you read the advice on the next page.

Rules for Treasure Hunters

Treasure hunting can prove to be a profitable undertaking. But if you decide to take it up there are certain rules you must obey:

1. Do not tamper with archeological sites or ancient monuments. You could do a great deal of damage and be liable to prosecution.

2. Report all finds of silver or gold to the police.

3. If you find live amunition or anything that could be dangerous, mark its position and report it to the police.

4. Report any unusual historical finds to your local museum.

5. Get permission from the owner before searching on private land.

6. Respect the country code. Do not damage plants or crops, close gates behind you, and do not leave any mess.

Light and Shade

If you are good at making things why not try making and selling lampshades? If you do, don't tell your friends you are in a shady business. It may be some time before they actually see the light!

It is best to start with reasonably simple cylindrical or cube-shaped frames. You can progress to more involved shapes when you have gained experience.

You will need: lampshade frames (from a handicraft shop but many large stores also sell them), covering materials, trimmings, glue, cottons.

The first stage of making simple lampshades is to make a paper pattern using the frame as a guide. The pattern is then fixed loosely around the frame to make sure it is the correct size and shape.

You now use the paper pattern to cut the material to the correct size.

Before the material can be attached to the frame, either by glueing or sewing, the frame should be prepared. There are two main ways of doing this: the first is to apply lacquer to the wires and the second is to cover the wires of the frame with bias binding.

If you are a really switched-on person, lampshade making could be a bright business for you.

Selling lampshades is a shady business

Money Problems

A good business person must always be able to solve problems. To do this requires practice so here are a few puzzles to tax your wits and provide you with the practice you need.

Purse Poser

There are five coins of equal value in a purse. How can you divide the coins equally between five people so that each person receives a coin? Easy—yes, but there is just one snag—you are also required to have one coin remaining in the purse. Now how do you do it?

Five by Four

Arrange ten coins on a table as shown. The dotted lines show there are three ways in which you can count four coins in a straight line. Can you now change the position of just two of the coins so that you have five straight lines each of four coins?

How Many?

Some coins are laid on a table. There are two coins in front of a coin, two coins behind a coin, and one coin in the centre. How many coins are there altogether?

In Your Pocket

You have two coins in your pocket amounting to 15p. If one of the coins is not a 5p piece what is the value of each of the two coins?

Bottle Off

Place a coin on a table. Now put a small bottle on top of the coin. Can you now get the bottle off the coin without touching either the coin or the bottle, without using a stick or anything else, and without getting someone else to do it for you?

coin →

Coin Cross

Place six coins on the table to form the cross formation shown. Can you now rearrange the coins so they form two straight rows each of four coins?

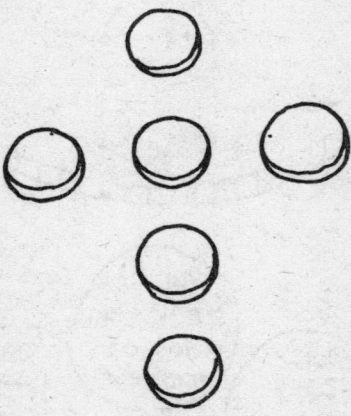

Answers on page 128.

Money, Money, Money

If you start from the letter M in the centre of this coin and then move from letter to letter moving either horizontally or vertically (but not diagonally) you can spell the word "money" in several ways. How many can you find?

Answers on page 128.

How to Buy a Village

You might think that the various jobs mentioned in this book are too ordinary to develop into successful businesses, but this is far from the case. True, not everyone who tries these ideas will become a millionaire. A lot of people should, however, be able to make a reasonable amount of money by trying one or more of the various schemes mentioned. It is quite possible to make a lot of money out of a business from which most people would make only small profits.

In 1977, June, Dickie, Bette and Nene Cessna who were aged between nine and thirteen, decided to start a little business venture. Although they did not have this book to guide them they decided to sell the horse manure from their father's stables. The business thrived and they made so much money that it was not long before they bought the stables for themselves!

Not satisfied with this success they continued to develop their business and by 1979 they had earned enough to buy their own village of Gorda, between Los Angeles and San Francisco. They paid £350,000 for the village and immediately began turning it into a recreation centre. If they continue with success in their business ventures there is no doubt that the four of them will be millionaires before very long.

Collecting for Charity

There are many ways of raising money for charity apart from just going from door to door and asking for it. If you wish to collect for charity, first contact the charity concerned to obtain their go-ahead and then try something like:

a bed race
a sponsored event (see page 125)
carol singing
collecting a penny for the guy
running a fete or a jumble sale (see page 120)
obtain a barrel from a brewery and then ask people to help you fill it with money
travel from Land's End to John O'Groats on a pogo stick

It is not even necessary to collect money, for a lot of charities will accept other things such as silver paper, stamps, newspapers, and so on. But before starting a collection write to the local branch of the charity (it should be in the telephone book) to see what they want. It is no good collecting a garage full of old bottles if the charity you wish to support wants only battered left shoes!

Life and Soul of the Party

People planning a party are always glad of additional help. You could provide this welcome assistance—for a fee, of course.

Among the things you could offer to do are: the washing up, cooking or preparing of food, entertainment (see page 68), organising games, acting as waiter or waitress, baby sitting (for adult parties), adult sitting (for children's parties!).

If you become involved in any jobs of an artistic or creative nature try to think up something different for each party you attend. If you offer your services as a games organiser, for example, you should have a wide range of games in your repertoire suitable for children of all ages. If you decide to be an entertainer it is as well to be able to change your programme occasionally for it is very likely that you will have much the same audience at any party in a given locality.

It is also possible to combine some of the services listed above. In addition to preparing the food you could also act as the waiter (or waitress), and do the washing up!

Running a Fête or Jumble Sale

Fêtes and jumble sales are good ways of raising money, particularly for charity. You can even hold them in your back garden and have a lot of fun in the process.

Fêtes

To run a really successful fête requires the co-operation of several people. Get them together several months before the event and decide what each person is going to do.

Stalls can be provided to sell old books, toys, clothes, ornaments — anything that friends or neighbours can either make or donate.

For large fêtes you can invite outside traders to set up their own stalls. Charge them a rent for the area and then any profit they make will be their own.

Drinks, sandwiches, biscuits, and cakes can be made by you and your helpers for sale on various stalls. It is a good idea to provide paper plates and cups for food and drink stalls. You will not then risk breaking your mum's best china and, better still, there will be no washing up to do.

Make sure you provide ample seating. Many of your visitors will simply want to chat to friends as they drink their lemonade and nibble on a fairy cake (both bought from your stalls of course).

Provide bins for rubbish — but be prepared for a lot of clearing up when everyone has gone.

In any organised event it is as well to have someone with a knowledge of first aid available. For a large fête ask the St. John's Ambulance or the Red Cross to attend in case of accidents. The police should also be notified if the fête is to be a large one.

To advertise your fête, make leaflets and push them through people's doors. Ask your local shopkeepers if they will put your leaflet in their window. And get as many people as you can to put one in the window of their car.

Competitions

Organise competitions and games to provide further attractions.

You could, for example, stage a wellie-throwing competition if there is enough room to stage the event. Make sure you first remove your wellies if you decide to offer them for this competition.

Here are some other ideas you could try:

Guess the weight of the cake. Contestants are allowed to lift the cake to get some idea of its weight (provided that it is not too heavy). The person who guesses closest to the actual weight wins the cake.

Guess the number of peas in a jar. In this case the winner does not win the jar of peas (unless he or she wants them) but some other more suitable prize.

    knobbly knees contest
    fancy dress contest
    guess the number of balloons in a car
    guess the number of spots on a dalmatian
    guess the number of beans in an unopened tin
    grandest (or most glamorous) granny contest

bonniest (not boniest) baby show
blindfold taste testing
obstacle race
quoits
a fortune teller

You could also feature games of skill such as:

darts
a coconut shy
hoop-la
throwing balls into a bucket

One word of warning: Any lottery or lucky draw is governed by the Lotteries and Amusements Act. You must ask at your local council offices for details of any restrictions that might apply to any form of competition you may have in mind.

Entertainment

If any of your friends can do an act you could put on an entertainment.

A separate charge can be made for the entertainment or it can be included in the entrance fee.

Your entertainment could consist of a talent competition. The entrants pay a small entry fee and the winner receives a prize. Judging can be done either by a panel of judges or by the amount of audience acclaim each performer receives.

It is a good idea to ask someone to perform the official opening of your fête. This does not have to be anyone famous but it is worthwhile asking someone who is well-known in the area.

With all events try to make some provision for bad weather. A jumble sale in the rain is a watery fête to be avoided.

Organising a jumble sale

Organising a jumble sale requires the same planning as for a fête. In addition to the things just mentioned you and your helpers will have to go around collecting the jumble.

Type some leaflets asking for donations of clothes, books, ornaments, and anything else that is saleable. Deliver these notices at least two weeks before your jumble sale. Several days later go from door to door to see what people have to offer — and don't forget you will need a car, a trolley, a cart, or a juggernaut to carry the items you collect.

The items you collect should be sorted and grouped together on tables. Have separate tables for children's clothing, adult clothing, toys, books, kitchen utensils, household items, and so on. Anything that cannot be conveniently grouped can be put together on one or more tables as bric-a-brac.

Try to put prices on as many items as you can as this will save haggling when someone wants to buy. Price tickets, cut from paper, can be pinned to clothing and tied or taped to other items. Book prices can be written on the inside cover of each book. Use a soft leaded pencil for this so it can be rubbed out easily. Try to keep your prices as low as possible and you will be more likely to sell everything.

Other events

All the ideas mentioned in this section are also applicable to other events such as gymkhanas, pet shows, athletics meetings, church bazaars, and so on.

Getting Yourself Sponsored

Sponsored events are a good way to raise money for charity, school funds, or to repair the church steeple. The idea is that your sponsors, anyone you can persuade to offer money, pay you a small amount for achieving something.

Usually sponsored events are of a sporting nature. How many lengths of the swimming pool you can swim before you drown is typical. But if you want to organise a sponsored event try to think of something that is a little out of the ordinary.

Here are a few ideas to get you thinking:

silence	how long can you remain silent?
spelling	a donation for each word you spell correctly — the words being selected by one of your teachers.
orange peeling	what is the longest continuous length of orange peel attained?
pea push	how many metres can you push a dried pea along the ground with your nose?
yo yo juggling	how long can you keep a yo yo going up and down?
no television	how long can you survive without watching the box?
car squash	how many people can you cram in a car?
bandaging	how quickly can you bandage a patient from head to toe?
longest kiss (ugh!)	make sure you pick someone you like if you get involved in this.
biggest bubble-gum bubble	blow up some bubble-gum until it splatters all over your face — the biggest bubble wins.
litter pick up	go through your town or village and see who can pick up the most rubbish.
three-legged race	it helps if you already have three legs.
joke-telling contest	what a laugh!

knitting knit-in   if your face is plain or your name is Pearl
you should be just the nit for this one.

Please remember that the police should be notified if you plan to organise a sponsored event in a public place or on the road.

When you have decided what the event is to be, the next step is to have some simple forms, like the one shown below.

Now you and your friends canvas family and neighbours to persuade them to donate a sum of money for each unit of the event that you complete successfully.

The sponsors write their name and address on the form together with the amount of their donation.

To make sure no-one cheats (as if they would!) there should be an adjudicator at the event. It is a good idea to have a local personality or someone respected in the locality to act as judge.

After the event and when each participant has had his or her achievement verified by the judge you go back to each sponsor to collect the amount due.

GRAND SPONSORED RUN
16 May 1983 at Fliptop Playing Fields

PARTICIPANT......... ADJUDICATOR.........

LAPS
COMPLETED .... SIGNED ....

NAME AND ADDRESS	AMOUNT PER LAP	TOTAL COLLECTED
	TOTAL	

Answers to Puzzles

SPOT THE FORGERY: Number 4 is the forgery.

FIT THEM IN:

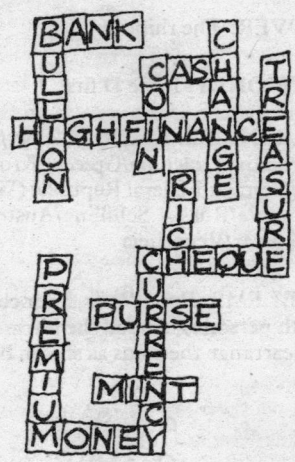

CURRENCY SEARCH:

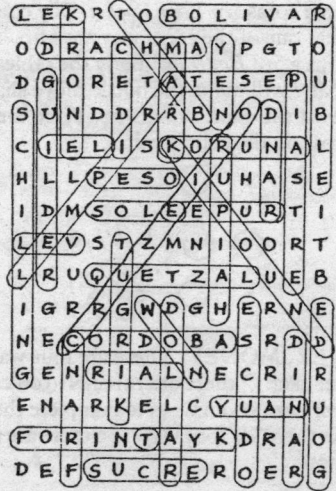

SPOT CHANGE: £1 on spine of second book; binding on fourth book; movement of right hand; safe handle; crease in money bag; Ivor Fortune's hair; spots on his nose; number of coins on table; button on coat sleeve; stripes on trousers.

COIN TURNOVER: The rhinoceros.

DESIGNS ON MONEY: Piece D fits.

WORLD CURRENCIES: Lire/Italy; Zloty/Poland; Guilder/Netherlands; Drachma/Greece; Krone/Denmark; Deutschemark/German Federal Republic (West Germany); Yuan/China; Rouble/Russia; Schilling/Austria; Yen/Japan; Kyat/Burma; Bolivar/Venezuela

MONEY PROBLEMS: *Purse Poser* Four coins are handed to four people. The fifth person is handed the purse with the coin still in it. *Five by Four* Rearrange the coins as shown below.

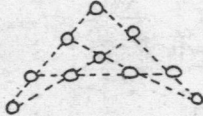

How Many: Three coins. *In Your Pocket* The coins are a 10p and a 5p. It was said that one of the coins was not a 5p. That's true — the other coin that was a 5p! *Bottle off* Bang the table top lightly with your fist. Each bang will make the bottle move slightly and it will eventually move off the coin. *Coin Cross* Place the coin from the bottom of the cross on the centre coin.

MONEY, MONEY, MONEY: There are four ways you can take from the M. After each O there are three Ns you can move to. From four Ns there are seven ways to complete the word and from the other eight Ns there are four ways. So there are at least sixty ways you can make 'money'.